DESTINED
TO
OVERCOME
THE TECHNIQUE
OF SPIRITUAL WARFARE

DESTINED TO OVERCOME

THE TECHNIQUE OF SPIRITUAL WARFARE

PAUL E. BILLHEIMER

BETHANY HOUSE PUBLISHERS

MINNEAPOLIS, MINNESOTA 55438

A Division of Bethany Fellowship, Inc.

Published by Bethany House Publishers
A Division of Bethany Fellowship, Inc.
6820 Auto Club Road, Minneapolis, Minnesota 55438

Printed in the United States of America

Library of Congress Cataloging in Publication Data

Billheimer, Paul E.
    Destined to overcome.

    Contents: The technique of spiritual warfare—Develop-
ing the personal prayer life—Turning on the switch—[etc.]
    1. Christian life—1960-   I. Title.

BV4501.2.B59   1982   248.4   82-4537

ISBN 0-87123-287-1 (pbk.)

The Author

PAUL E. BILLHEIMER has ministered for
Christ for more than sixty-one years. His previous
writings have sold many thousands of copies and
have been greatly blessed by God for the building
up of the Church. He and his wife now make their
home in California and work closely with the
Trinity Broadcasting Network.

By the same author

Destined for the Throne

Author Paul E. Billheimer, a former radio pastor and Bible college president, shares unique insights into God's purposes in the creation of the universe and the human race, illustrating the truth that "through the ages, one eternal purpose runs." This world is a laboratory in which those destined for the throne are learning in actual practice how to overcome Satan and his hierarchy.

Over half a million are in print in English, plus 24 foreign languages which are either in print or in process of translation.

Don't Waste Your Sorrows

From a different perspective, in this book the author deals with the question of suffering as an indispensable part of God's program of preparation and training of His children for ultimate participation in rulership as members of the Bride of Christ. Based on the same cosmology as his earlier volume, *Destined for the Throne*, the author here gives an eminently satisfying answer to the frequent question, "Why, Lord?"

There are 170,000 in print in English, plus several foreign languages.

Love Covers

Third in this trilogy, *Love Covers* promotes a viable platform for Christian unity. The main thesis of this book is that fellowship between all truly born-again believers should be upon a basis of a common origin, a common parentage, a common family relationship, rather than a common opinion concerning issues non-essential to salvation.

There are 100,000 in print.

Foreword

"And ye shall know the truth, and the truth shall set you free" (John 8:32).

Never in the history of the world has it been more important for the Christian warrior to know the truth of the Word of God and the authority we possess in Jesus Christ than at this moment in history. Far too often the child of God allows Satan to bluff, bluster and coerce him into submission and defeat when he has ready to aid him *all the power* of the resurrected, victorious Christ!

The problem? Lack of knowledge. "My people perish for lack of knowledge" (Hos. 4:6). Oh, that we might know how to use the Word of God as Jesus did when He defeated Satan with, *"It is written."*

Paul Billheimer has drawn from the Word of God "The Technique of Spiritual Warfare" which, if put into practice by the child of God, will turn defeat into victory, tragedy into triumph! I urge each reader to prayerfully study this writing with Bible in hand and then to go forth to devastate Satan's kingdom.

Praise God! We are "more than conquerors"

(Rom. 8:37)! Let us repossess all that Satan has stolen from us *now* in Jesus' name!

Paul F. Crouch
President
Trinity Broadcasting Network, Inc.

Preface

The Christian life is indeed a warfare. Unless we view it as such and learn the techniques of overcoming our adversary, we are going to live a life of defeat. The message found in Part I of *Destined to Overcome* was designed to assist the believer in recognizing his "weapons" and teach him some skills in using them effectively in every aspect of his prayer life. We need to know that God has made every provision for us to be *more than conquerors through Him that loved us and gave himself FOR US.*

"The Technique of Spiritual Warfare" was shared with our radio audience and published in our own publication in the year 1952. It is here reproduced, with slight modifications, as it was released almost thirty years ago. Because it was controversial then, and according to some, it may be now, a letter from Dr. F. J. Huegel is attached. Dr. Huegel was a lifelong missionary to Mexico and is the well-known author of *Bone of His Bone, The Cross of Christ—The Throne of God,* and many other spiritual classics. His letter was unsolicited and was received shortly after this message was first published:

Mexico D.F.

Dear Friend and Brother in Christ our Lord:

Our friendship has deep roots, although we do not often write to each other. I have just been reading "The Technique of Spiritual Warfare," and it has brought you forcibly before me. My heart cries "Amen" to every word, Dear brother, and I pray the Lord that He might bless you more and more as you seek to bring to light these great truths that have to do with the victory of Calvary and the authority of the believer as the result thereof. The dear Lord, through much suffering, has for many years now been teaching me to lay hold of these weapons which are not carnal but mighty through God for the pulling down of Satan's strongholds.

I like your thought of a "permanent" binding of the enemy, that is, on the basis of the shed blood of our blessed Redeemer, to command evil spirits to go back to the abyss and stay there permanently, as you put it.

I have recently been visiting in Central and South America in an effort to get these principles across to the pastors and missionaries. According to my view of missions, their greatest need today is to get a clear-cut vision of the Calvary victory and a knowledge of the technique of its enforcement. Oh, what it would mean to the church and to the world if Christians would lay hold of these weapons.

Zondervan is publishing a new work of mine, a message which the Lord gave me, under the title FOREVER TRIUMPHANT. This message goes into the analysis of these principles.

Yours fraternally in the bonds of Calvary,
(Signed) F. J. Huegel

Part II, "Developing the Personal Prayer Life," was written under this title at the invitation of the Program Committee for the American Festival of Evangelism which convened in Kansas City, July 27-30, 1981. It was my privilege to deliver this message in one of the workshops of that historic gathering of spiritual leaders.

While many cardinal truths contained in *Destined for the Throne* concerning the theology of prayer are incorporated in this message, there is much additional teaching that is vital to the successful prayer life of the believer.

Prayer is a warfare. We need to understand some basic theology of successful praying in order to use our weapons effectively. This message fits hand-in-hand with the message of Part I, "The Technique of Spiritual Warfare" as a handbook for the intercessor.

In the mid to late thirties when our radio ministry began, there was comparatively little teaching on faith for divine healing. I had been healed from terminal tuberculosis about ten years previously and only through diligent study of the Word, prayer, and two or three available books on the subject had I come into some kind of a theology of faith for healing. The subject was new to most of our listeners and multitides were hungry for teaching from the Word. Part III of this book, "Turning on the Switch," was a part of a continued daily radio teaching along this line in the early part of 1939 and was published in our little paper, *Christ for Soul and Body*. These principles have continued as a part of our "faith furniture" for more than forty years. We still find them valid and effective. The message is presented here with only very minor editorial corrections.

We hear from many people who say, "I believe in divine healing. I am thoroughly convinced that it is God's will to heal today and even to heal me, but I do not know how to appropriate faith; I do not know how to take it." The purpose of this series of broadcasts is to assist you to do this very thing. If you will follow closely step by step, keeping your heart open and fully obeying all instructions given, I believe that you will be able to exercise faith for your healing before this subject is concluded.

Contents

PART ONE

The Technique of Spiritual Warfare

The Problem

Humanity is beset by a host of self-conscious evil spirit personalities called demons who are responsible for much, if not most, of the personality difficulties, complexities, spiritual pressures, strains and the aggravated forms of evil that characterize our modern social order.

The fallen condition of mankind, the sin of the human heart alone, does not explain the abnormal psychoses and the universal snarling and fouling of human relations. This constant and fiendish disruption of the human social order is explained only by the mass activity behind the scenes of a vast, well-organized host of wicked

21

spirits under the control of their master prince. Any spiritual method or technique which ignores the presence and activity of these occult forces cannot possibly offer an adequate solution for the problems plaguing mankind.

Solution

When once the technique of overcoming is understood, it can be used effectively no matter what form the demon activity may assume. God's method of overcoming is specifically set forth in Revelation 12:11. After describing the war in heaven and the expulsion of Satan and his angels into the earth, the writer explains that in the warfare set up against the brethren as a result of Satan's expulsion, the victory was won by *"the blood of the Lamb* and *the word of their testimony."*

In this apparently incidental reference, the Holy Spirit has handed to the discerning saint weapons of supreme effectiveness in this spiritual warfare. This reference is on first glance so casual that its implications are in danger of being overlooked. In it is contained all that the truly yielded saint needs for triumphant warfare.

Calvary—Defeat or Victory?

The reference to "the blood of the Lamb" is a

direct reference to Calvary and the victory which was there won over the arch foe of God and man. In order to use effectively the weapon of the blood, it is absolutely necessary to understand what actually took place at Calvary. To the natural mind Calvary was a defeat. To the ordinary man of the world, Calvary looks like a victory for Satan.

I can remember yet how I used to wish that Jesus had silenced the taunts of the Scribes and Pharisees by coming down from the cross and thus "proving" that He was the Son of God. In order to understand what actually happened at Calvary, one must understand first what happened at the Fall in the Garden of Eden.

Man was originally made for authority. He was created and fashioned for dominion. When he came fresh from the hand of God, he was given rulership of the earth, kingship of its life, and the control and mastery of its forces. In Genesis 1:26 it is recorded, "And God said, let us make man in our image, after our likeness; and let them have dominion over the fish of the sea, and over the fowl of the air, and over the cattle, and over all the earth, and over every creeping thing that creepeth upon the earth." The writer of the 8th Psalm states specifically, "Thou madest him to have dominion over the works of thy hand: thou has put *all* things under his feet."

A Bona Fide Grant

This granting of authority and dominion over

the earth to man was a bona fide grant. God gave the dominion of the entire earth to man. It was his to do with as he should decide to do. God did not give the earth to man with certain strings attached. What man did with that dominion and authority was his own responsibility. If man "fumbled the ball," so to speak, God would not step in and forcibly reposses His gift. I repeat, *it was a bona fide gift.*

All of us are familiar with the story of the Fall, but not all of us understand how it affected man's rulership over the earth. When man at the time of the Fall transferred his allegiance from God to Satan, he also transferred his dominion.

Since the rulership of this earth was a true gift from God to man, man had the legal right to do with that dominion what he chose. Because it was given to man, the rulership of this world was no longer under God's direct control, for He gave it to man. And then it was not man's, for he gave it to Satan. Satan became, therefore, the legal and actual ruler of this world. This is why Satan is characterized in the Scripture as "the god of this world," and "the prince of this world," and "the prince of the power of the air." The kingship, the rulership of this earth which originally was given to man, legally became Satan's.

A Legal Issue

Why did God not go over man's head and forcibly take the dominion away from Satan and keep it himself? There is a very important legal issue involved. If God had done that, He would have been violating legal principles which were part of His Creation and a direct expression of His nature. If God had gone over man's head and taken the dominion by force away from Satan, that would have been to repossess it without "due process of law," a violation of divine justice. For God has bound himself to observe principles of divine jurisprudence even where Satan, the "father of lies," is concerned. God cannot be unjust even with Satan.

Man's Bondage to Satan

Because man transferred the title for the dominion of this earth to Satan, the only way God could legally recover it for man was through man, the original trustee of the earth.

The earth was given to man. It was swung away from God and away from man's dominion by man's choice. It must be swung back by man. But where was the man who could do this?

When Adam's allegiance went from God to Satan and with it the dominion of the world, man ceased to be free and became a slave of Satan. Being owned and controlled by Satan, he could in no way free himself. A man must be found upon whom Satan had no claim or control in order to head a movement for swinging the world back to its original allegiance. This man must be able to remove Satan's legal claim to the earth before it could be restored to its original rulership.

This man had to be a member of the trustee group in order to qualify to enter the legal battle to repossess the earth, God's gift to man. And he had to be without stain or taint of sin. He had to be absolutely perfect in order not to furnish Satan with any legal claim upon him. He could not be Adam's son, for then he would have Adam's taint; and if he had Adam's taint he could not live a perfect life. And if he did not live a perfect life he would be Satan's slave like all of the rest.

If he were not perfectly human, one of the trustees, he would not be qualified for entering the legal battle. If he were not divine, very God of very God, he could not live a perfect life and would therefore come under the control of Satan and be put out of the battle. Everything depended upon these two factors.

Anyone's claims that it makes no difference whether Jesus was divine or not are the result either of malice afore thought or criminally loose thinking. He has either a bad heart or a weak head, or both. If Christ is not the son of Mary and the Son of God by virtue of a supernatural conception, then He was the son of Mary and Joseph and inherited Adam's disposition to sin with all the rest of us. If He inherited Adam's sin, He was Satan's slave; and if He was Satan's slave, then

He was both legally and morally disqualified to enter the battle.

A Qualified Representative

But Jesus came, a man among men. And when He appeared, a mighty battle took place between Christ and Satan. All the destiny of the world and of the human race depended upon the outcome of this battle. If Satan could find or produce one tiny flaw in the life and character of this Man, then he, Satan, would control Him and remain the undisputed ruler of the world and the human race.

In the long conflict from Bethlehem to Calvary, the most terrific battle ever waged, the actual and only righful Heir to the throne of dominion and the false pretender to that throne were locked in mortal combat. Through thirty-three years, that warfare continued with unabated intensity. The fallen "son of the morning," the highest of all pre-adamic created beings, marshalled all of his subtlety and power to break down the allegiance of this God-Man to His heavenly Father. One weakness revealed, one fatal flaw, and all His efforts to repossess the world and its enslaved race from the usurping prince would be lost.

This usurping prince did his best and worst during those Nazareth years, later in the temptation in the wilderness, in the years of ministry, in the Garden of Gethsemane and, finally, ~~clear up to~~ Calvary. He made every effort to secure a breakdown in His allegiance to God and a transfer of that allegiance to Satan. That was his object in the wilderness when he tempted Him to fall down and worship him. But Jesus was victorious there. He defeated him with the Word, "Thou shalt worship the Lord thy God, and him only shalt thou serve" (Matt. 4:10). That was Satan's object in Gethsemane, but again Jesus triumphed when He said, "Nevertheless not my will, but thine, be done" (Luke 22:42).

Satan's object in bringing Christ to the cross was to compel Him to rebel against the will of the Father, and, therefore, transfer His allegiance to Satan. This archfiend of darkness pushed Jesus clear up to death, "even the death of the cross." In other words, Jesus submitted to death, "even the death of the cross," without having one thought out of harmony with His heavenly Father. Satan's real purpose in all of his cruel attacks and pressure upon Jesus was to compel Him to fail just once in His submission to God. This is the meaning of all that befell Jesus ~~clear~~ up to Gethsemane and the cross.

When at last Jesus bowed His head and died without once failing in His submission to His heavenly Father, *Satan was defeated* in the conflict. Satan's great purpose, to produce in Jesus

one small thought of rebellion against His Father,
came to naught when Jesus died without yielding
to that temptation. He triumphed even though
the death seemed to be a defeat.

Satan's Defeat

The death of Jesus without His failing in one of
the smallest details resulted not only in defeating
Satan's purpose to obtain a claim upon Jesus, but
it also cancelled all of Satan's claims upon the
earth and the entire human race.

Under human jurisprudence, when a man
slays another man, he himself becomes subject to
the death penalty. In other words, when someone
murders an innocent person, he forfeits his own
life, he destroys himself. This is a fundamental
concept of divine law, as given in Genesis 9:6,
"Whoso sheds man's blood, by man shall his
blood be shed." Since human jurisprudence, inso-
far as it comes from God, is only a reflection of the
divine, it is easy to see what happened to Satan
when he pushed Jesus clear up to the cross in his
effort to compel Him to rebel against His Father.
When Jesus dismissed His Spirit without giving
Satan any claim upon Him, Satan became the
murderer of an innocent victim upon whom he
had no claim; he therefore became subject, in the
court of universal justice, to the death penalty.
Satan's rebellion against God "from before the

world was" finally brought him to the crime of crimes—his conspiracy with demons and evil men to kill God.

Jesus said, "I lay down my life for the sheep. . . . No man taketh it from me, but I lay it down of myself" (John 10:15, 18). The devil did not know that he was merely an instrument in bringing about the death for all mankind which God had intended from the beginning. Satan did not realize that his ultimate insurrection against God was signing his own death sentence.

Satan had slain his millions before this time with impunity, because he had a claim upon them. When this one who had the power of death exercised it upon others, he was only doing what he wanted to with that which was his own. Because a slave owner has legal title to all the offspring of his slave, Satan had legal title to all of Adam's sons and could do with them as he wished. But he who had the power of death and had exercised it upon helpless millions of his slaves, now committed the most colossal blunder of his age-long career. In his desperate effort to compel Jesus to break with His heavenly Father, he slew an innocent Man, One upon whom he had no claim. And in so doing, he brought upon himself the penalty of death—he destroyed himself. This is what the author of the Letter to the Hebrews means when he said, "that through death he might destroy him that had the power of death, that is, the devil" (2:14).

If this means anything, it means that when Satan slew the innocent Son of God, he destroyed himself. If this means anything, it means that Satan is now destroyed— not annihilated, but *destroyed*. All of the legal claims which he secured upon the earth and man through Adam's Fall are now completely cancelled; since the cross, he has absolutely no right at all upon any one or any thing. It means that all the power which he exercises now he exercises solely by deception and bluff.

This is the basis for Jesus' statement in Matthew 28:18: "All power [authority] is given unto me in heaven and in earth." This is also the basis for His delegation of that authority in Luke 10:19: "Behold, I give unto you power [authority] to tread on serpents and scorpions [demons], and over all the power of the enemy: and nothing shall by any means hurt you."

Satan on the Loose.

If all of this is true, if Satan is actually destroyed, why is it that Satan continues to run things? Why is it that almost everything looks as if it is in his control? Why is it that he seems to be the governing factor in human life and affairs? He is having his way with almost everything. If he is destroyed, if all his claims are cancelled, why, then, is this so?

Many of us have had our honest doubts as to whether Calvary was really a victory or a defeat. It looks to the human mind as if almost everything is going to the devil. We cannot reconcile the teaching that Christ is triumphant with what we see going on around us. Common sense and realism gives rise to the sickening suspicion that the supremacy of Christ in the universe is a gigantic hoax or myth. If Jesus actually destroyed Satan upon the cross, if Calvary is actually a victory, why don't we see more evidence of it in human life and world affairs?

The Question of Enforcement

The answer is this: Legally, Calvary was Satan's complete undoing. Legally, the Cross completely destroyed Satan. All of his claims were cancelled when he sent Jesus to the cross and He died there. But like any other legal transaction, *Calvary's legal victory must be enforced.*

It may be illustrated this way: In our Federal Government, for instance, there are three departments: the Legislative department, which is Congress, passes the laws; the Judicial, which is the Courts, interprets them; and the Executive, which is headed by the President, is charged with the duty of enforcing them. The Legislative never enforces the law. The Judiciary never enforces the law. This is the sole responsibility of the executive agency. If the executive fails to enforce the statutes, they become a dead letter. No matter how legal a measure is, no matter how it has been interpreted by the court as constitutional, unless the executive enforces the law, it is competely nullified; it is all the same as if it were not a legal measure.

All of us know what happened to the 18th Amendment. It was indeed the law of the land. It stood all the tests of Constitutionality. But its enforcement was entrusted to Andrew Mellon, then secretary of the Treasury, head of one of the largest brewing syndicates in the world. It became a dead letter through non-enforcement.

This is an illustration of what happens in the matter of Satan's legal destruction. Calvary was indeed a victory. It in actual fact destroyed all of Satan's legal claims. Nothing is lacking there. But the enforcement of Calvary's victory was placed in the hands of the Church, Christ's corporate Body upon earth. The Body with hands and feet is the vehicle which carries out the commands of the Head. If the Body fails to respond, the will of the Head becomes a dead letter.

The Constitutional Basis of the Believer's Authority

The authority to enforce Christ's victory over

Satan was delegated to the Church in Matthew 16:18, 19: "And I say also unto thee, That thou art Peter, and upon this rock I will build my church; and the gates of hell shall not prevail against it. And I will give unto thee the keys of the kingdom of heaven; and whatsoever thou shalt bind on earth shall be bound in heaven: and whatsoever thou shalt loose on earth shall be loosed in heaven." Also in Matthew 18:18, "Verily I say unto you, Whatsoever ye shall bind on earth shall be bound in heaven: and whatsoever ye shalt loose on earth shall be loosed in heaven."

This divine mandate is confirmed in Luke 10:17-19: "And the seventy returned again with joy, saying, Lord, even the devils [demons] are subject unto us through thy name. And he said unto them, I beheld Satan as lightning fall from heaven. Behold, I give unto you power to tread on serpents and scorpions, and over all the power of the enemy: and nothing shall by any means hurt you."

This delegation of authority is further clearly implied in Matthew 28:18, 19: "And Jesus came and spake unto them, saying, All power is given unto me in heaven and on earth. Go ye therefore . . . "—all power (authority) was given unto Jesus by virtue of His triumph which was consummated at Calvary. In turn, He has delegated that authority to His disciples. These Scriptures form a solid basis for their commission as the agents of enforcement of Calvary's victory.

Failure of the Enforcement Agency

The fact that Satan seems to be having his way is no reflection upon the genuineness of Christ's victory over Satan at the cross. It means only that the enforcement agency has failed. If we realized what actually happened to Satan at Calvary, if we understood the utterness of his defeat, if we comprehended the power of the blood and the effectiveness of our authority, our own experience and the world's history might have been different.

Satan has succeeded in keeping God's people in the dark about what happened to him at the cross. By brainwashing and deception, he has succeeded in convincing the Church that he is almost, if not quite, as powerful as God, when actually he has no power at all. He has no legal standing, no rights, no authority. He knows that when the Church fully realizes the utterness of his defeat and how to use the authority which has been delegated to her, he is done for. Therefore, he hopes God's people will stay in the dark, not knowing or using the authority which is theirs.

The Apprenticeship of Prayer

Some have Satan-inspired misgivings about spending time in the ministry of prayer, because they do not understand why God works only through prayer. His object in originating His prayer program was to *give us training for overcoming* in preparation for rulership. He is using it as an apprenticeship. He did not devise prayer as merely His unique way of getting things done. In His plan, prayer has only one purpose—to give us exercise in overcoming.

God has the power to accomplish all His other purposes without our cooperation in prayer except our need for training and education. He has no other way of training us for rulership except by our cooperation in prayer. For this reason He does nothing in the realm of human redemption except through prayer. *He has tied all of his activity and accomplishment to prayer.* All that He does in this field is limited to the prayers of His people.

Prayer is not answered on the basis of worthiness. Because no one who prays is absolutely morally perfect, (many are far from moral perfection) *the crucial factor in getting answers to prayer is not primarily spiritual superiority but simply the boldness, courage and faith to pray regardless of our sense of unworthiness.* If we are conscientiously walking in the light God has given, we are never to permit a sense of unworthiness to hamper our prayer life; this is made clear in Hebrews 4:15, 16: "For we have not an high priest which cannot be touched with the feeling of our infirmities; but was in all points tempted like as we are, yet without sin. Let us therefore come boldly to the throne of grace, that we may obtain mercy, and find grace to help in time of need."

God knows all about our weaknesses, frailties and unworthiness; because He was tempted in exactly the same way, He knows exactly how unworthy we feel, yet He invites us to come anyway. He invites us to come boldly, not because we are worthy but because *He is worthy*. He has planned that prayer be an apprenticeship, a learning experience to prepare us for rulership in the ages to come.

On-the-Job Training

Many of us feel that God will answer prayer only for other people, especially for those whom we believe to be spiritually superior. This is because we have "inside information" concerning our own weaknesses, infirmities, unworthiness and sin. While it is true that "If I regard iniquity in my heart, God will not hear me," all prayers which are heard and answered are heard and answered for one reason and one alone: *because of what Christ has done for us.*

When we accept Christ as our Savior and are born again, for that very reason God credits all of Christ's worthiness to us. If you doubt this, see 1 Corinthians 1:30 (NIV): "It is because of Him that you are in Christ Jesus, who has become for us wisdom from God—that is our righteousness, holiness and redemption"—the finished work. This is why all prayer that is heard and answered must be made in His name, that is, on the basis of *His* worthiness, not ours.

If you are born again, walking in all the light you have, not tolerating any known sin, *you are as eligible for answers to your prayers as the most mature saint.* The only requirement is that you pray. "Ye have not because ye ask not " (James 4:2).

Because prayer is "on-the-job training," God's purpose in inaugurating the system of prayer cannot be realized apart from prayer. "Ye have not," not because of your unworthiness but simply because you do not ask. Satan uses your feeling of unworthiness to prevent your praying. When he succeeds, he has won.

All the prayers that God is answering are from people who not only feel unworthy as you do, but who actually *are* unworthy. God does all His work through unworthy people, who, despite a conviction of unworthiness, are making prayer the main business of their lives anyway. Therefore, do not permit Satan to brainwash you and stymie you any more because of your sense of unworthiness.

If you are close enough to God for Him to lay a burden of prayer upon you, you are qualified to pray, to be an intercessor. The time you spend in prayer is not wasted.

All prayer that is according to God's will originates in the heart of God. When God lays a burden of prayer upon you, it means that He is already at work to accomplish it. Therefore, when you have a God-given burden for *anything*, you can pray in faith that God is already in action.

Do not any longer permit Satan to frighten you out of prayer because of a sense of unworthiness. You have been given authority over Satan, but this authority is totally useless if you do not pray.

Authority in the Spoken Word

As we have stated, spiritual authority is legally based upon "the blood of the Lamb"—that is, the victory of Calvary. Understanding and knowing what actually happened at the cross, realizing why and how Satan was destroyed and his claims cancelled by Christ's death, are absolutely essential to the next step in overcoming: "And they overcame him by the blood of the Lamb, and by the word of their testimony" (Rev. 12:11).

For years I thought this "word of testimony" referred to a testimony of the goodness of God as is customary in prayer and praise services. But the time came when the Spirit began to reveal that this testimony was a word spoken directly to Satan and his demon spirits in the Name of Jesus and upon the basis of His shed blood; a command to them, spoken in the first person. I was hesitant to accept this position since I had no precedent to follow. I had never heard, so far as I can remember, any one else so interpret this Scripture—speaking the word of command directly to Satan and his emissaries. Satan sought to frighten me in order to prevent my attempting such a thing. He tried to tell me that something terrible would happen to me if I became so presumptuous as to speak to him directly, even in the Name of Jesus of Nazareth and upon the basis of His shed blood.

But I remembered that Jesus himself spoke directly to Satan. "Get thee behind me, Satan" (Matt. 16:23) was His response when Peter allowed himself to be an instrument of the devil. At the time of His temptation in the wilderness, He said, "Get thee hence, Satan: for it is written . . . " (Matt. 4:10). And James exhorts us to "resist the devil, and he will flee from you" (4:7). Since Satan does not have a body and cannot be attacked physically, this resistance must take the form of a verbal assault—not in our own power or strength or wisdom but *in the Name of Jesus!* When at last in hesitation, in fear and trembling, I ventured to speak directly to him; calling him by name; commanding him and his demons of depression, oppression, affliction and bondage, in the Name of Jesus of Nazareth and upon the basis of His shed blood, to leave me and release me, *I discovered immediate release and relief.* It was as though the demons of doubt, fear and bondage instantly melted at the Name of Jesus and the blood of the Lamb when the word of command was spoken directly to them. Now, with the word of my testimony, I declared aloud that they had been destroyed by Christ's death and that their claims were cancelled, that they had no right whatever to touch me, that they were trespassers when they attempted to do so. When I did this, commanding them in the Name of Jesus to go, I experienced immediate relief and freedom.

A Fleeing Satan

Many believers have been so tyrannized and dominated by Satan and the prevailing theology of Satan's power and invincibility that, like me, they would never dare to speak directly to him, even in the name of Jesus. For years, I couldn't imagine Satan running away. The picture that had frightened and terrified me was of Satan on the attack, "going about like a roaring lion, seeking whom he may devour" (1 Peter 5:8). James' exhortation to resist encouraged me to face that roaring lion. When I mustered enough courage to speak directly to him in the name of Jesus, it was a great surprise to me to discover an immediate sense of deliverance—as though he had vanished, melted away.

Jesus, after giving us authority over all the power of the enemy, (Luke 10:19) reassured us by saying "nothing shall by any means hurt you." I needed that reassurance.

It was with great caution that I attempted carefully to share this secret with others. Then I discovered an article by Mrs. Jessie Penn Lewis, "Overcoming the Accuser." As I read this message my own convictions were clarified and confirmed. When I more boldly began to share this secret with our radio audience, people began to write in immediately and testify that "it works." As a result, many of the Lord's people have confirmed the effectiveness of this technique. They have given witness to glorious deliverance from afflictions and bondages of all kinds, many times bondages of life-time duration.

The Importance of Being Specific

In order to experience the power in the blood of Christ and the word of our testimony or command, it is important to be very literal and specific. You must first of all recognize the source and origin of your difficulties. I believe we shall discover that far more of our troubles than we have ever dreamed are the result of the interference with body, mind and spirit by demon personalities under the command of Satan as their prince. I am convinced that much oppression which we attribute to natural causes such as disposition, temperament, moods, fear and depression is demon inspired. *There is no such thing as abstract evil. Evil always has an intelligent, self-conscious source. There is no evil that does not originate in a personality.*

Evil spirits seem to have some access to thought processes. At least, from years of seeing our reaction, watching our responses, noting what we say, the devil no doubt has a fairly accurate idea of what a person is thinking at a given moment. He knows how to "ride into" our thought on the wave of circumstances, influencing our thoughts and insinuating his own interpretation of situations.

But I do not believe that we can address Satan directly through our thought. The only way we can be sure that he knows we are resisting him is to *speak aloud,* to directly and audibly confront him with the truth.

May I remind you again that *our resistance* by itself is not what causes Satan to flee; he flees because of the *power of Jesus* which is ours through prayer.

"The very weapons we use are not those of human warfare but powerful in God's warfare for the destruction of the enemy's strongholds. Our battle is to bring down every deceptive fantasy and every imposing defense that men erect against the knowledge of God. We even fight to capture every thought until it acknowledges the authority of Christ" (1 Cor. 10:4, 5, Phillips).

One Devil—Many Demons

Fear is one of Satan's greatest weapons. In my years of ministry, I have known many who have been bound by ungodly fears—fear of failure, fear of acceptance, fear of loneliness, fear of pain— and, yes, fear of the devil. The Bible clearly warns us about Satan—not in order that we will fear him but so that we will know how to overcome him.

I encourage you to speak to your fears: "Thou demon of fear, in the Name of Jesus I bind you and command you to be removed and cast into the abyss." You may find that speaking to your fears is more effective than much counselling by others.

We must remember that Satan is the ruler over an immense kingdom, a vast hierarchy of wicked spirits through whom he carries on his work. That is the meaning of Ephesians 6:12: "For ours is not a conflict with mere flesh and blood, but with the despotisms, the empires, the forces that control and govern this dark world— the spiritual hosts of evil arrayed against us in the heavenly warfare" (Weymouth). Concerning this, Dr. Bob Jones says, "The devil has a tremendous army—the devil probably doesn't know some of you folks but he has some representatives that do know you. He is not omnipresent. He is not everywhere at the same time—but he has a great host of demons—a mighty army.

Nor is Satan omnipotent or omniscient; he has to carry on his work through demons. Just as God has "angels who are sent forth as ministering spirits to minister to those who shall be heirs of salvation" (Heb. 1:14), so Satan has his wicked spirits whom, I believe, he sends forth to plague, oppress, and afflict all humanity, especially those who seek to escape his snares.

The Personality of Evil Spirits

These evil spirits are self-conscious personalities who can hear and see and think and feel. Remember the story of Jesus casting the evil spirits out of the man in the country of the Gadarenes? The spirits begged Jesus not to torment them, showing emotions of fear and calling themselves by a specific name, Legion. They have all the attributes of personality except a body.

In ways which we may not fully understand, they have power to interfere with bodily functions: "Ought not this woman . . . whom Satan hath bound . . . be loosed?" (Luke 13:16), to oppress the mind and the spirit and, in general, to distort human personality. When our trouble, whether mental, physical, or spiritual, is the result of demon activity, the technique of overcoming set forth in Revelation 12:11 will certainly bring relief.

When you discover that your trouble is the result of satanic or demonic oppression, try speaking directly to the demon or demons, calling them by name and commanding them in the Name of Jesus and upon the basis of Calvary's victory to release you, to take their hands off and go back to the abyss, and stay there.

Some people will object to commanding them to stay there permanently, and I am offering this to you for what it is worth. I am not dogmatic about it, but I have discovered a permanence of relief and victory which I did not have until I followed these demons clear through. And with the blood of Jesus, sealed them permanently in the depths of the abyss.

God Shall Bruise Satan

I realize that this will seem to many to be the rankest fanaticism, and I do not ask anyone to accept it who does not feel it is biblical. I am not advancing this as dogmatic truth. I only submit it with these reasons: First of all, as I have said, I have found a new victory myself in commanding them to go back to the abyss and stay there.

Second, there is the truth found in Matthew 16:18 and 18:18: "Whatsoever thou shalt bind on earth, shall be bound in heaven." I cannot believe that God would wish these evil spirits who are plaguing the people of God to be bound only temporarily. I cannot believe that God wants anything less than permanent deliverance. We know that the abyss is their final destination and that Jesus shed His blood to put them there. Can we doubt that He wishes any delay in the final triumph of the Cross over them?

Again, if the Church is the enforcement agency into whose hands the enforcement of the victory of Calvary is entrusted, may it not be that Christ's final triumph over Satan and the incarceration of the powers of evil awaits aggressive action by the Church, awakened to its rightful authority? Paul said, "The God of peace shall bruise Satan under your feet shortly" (Rom. 16:20). And can anyone doubt that God's plans and purposes would not be enhanced by the actual beginning to bind the satanic hosts and cast them into the abyss now?

Back to the story of the demons of Gadara (Matt. 8:29, Mark 5, Luke 8), they pleaded with Jesus not to torment them before their time, not to send them into the abyss; and, apparently, He granted their request. This passage indicates that the abyss is their final doom. We may not know why Jesus did this, but some Bible students suggest that the entrance to the abyss may be in the sea. Could it be that, after all, when the pigs went down into the sea, they were actually carrying the demons into the abyss?

We may not know where demons actually go when they are cast out of people. Personally, I would be more comfortable if I knew they were not around where they could harass other people. And as the governing factor in the world, may it not be that God is waiting for His people to seize and exercise the authority that He has delegated to them before His plan can move into its final stages?

I do not affirm, I only raise questions. I am not speaking or writing for those who have a doctrine to maintain or a theological system to defend, but for those who long to enter into God's secret purposes and plans and who long to see Calvary's victory enforced. If there are those who feel I do not have sufficient Scripture to support my position in attempting to condemn evil spirits to the abyss now, I have no controversy with you.

This thought, however, was not wholly unknown to Paul, for he tells us in 1 Corinthians 6:2, 3, "Do ye not know that the saints will judge angels?" and Paul's word in Romans that God would bruise Satan under their feet shortly. Without doubt this refers to the judgment of evil angels or demons. And who has a right to say that that judgment may not begin now on the part of those who are able to exercise the authority that Christ has delegated to believers?

While I am not dogmatic about this matter for others, I feel justified in refusing to allow myself to be cheated out of the victory which I have experienced; I will continue to follow through and place the permanent seal of the blood upon those whom I command to release their victims and go back to the abyss. And I am not alone is this; many others have testified to definite relief by this method.

The Powerful Word of Command

When one understands that evil spirits are self-conscious personalities who hear and see and feel and think, it becomes clear why the word of command in the Name of Jesus is effective. Evidently this is what the centurion had in mind in Luke 7:6, 8:"And when he was now not far from the house, the centurion sent friends to him, saying unto him, Lord, trouble not thyself; for I am not worthy that thou shouldest enter under my roof: wherefore neither thought I myself worthy to come unto thee; but say in a word, and my servant shall be healed. For I also am a man set under authority, having under me soldiers, and I say unto one, Go, and he goeth; and to another, Come, and he cometh; and to my servant, Do this, and he doeth it."

This Roman centurion showed more insight into spiritual things than did the Jews or many modern believers. Back of this statement is an amazing awareness of what goes on in the invisible world. The centurion is convinced that his servant is afflicted by evil spirits. He is also convinced that these evil spirits are subject to the authority of Jesus. But that authority has to be expressed by a word, a word of command, just as the authority of the centurion himself is expressed by his word of command. When the centurion says "Go," those under his authority obey. He reasons, therefore, that all Jesus needs to do is to speak the word, since words are the medium by which resident authority is transmitted. Again, thought or wish alone is not sufficient.

The Dynamic of Speech

The universe was created not by thought but by speech. "He spake, and it was done; he commanded, and it stood fast" (Psa. 33:9). Without doubt, from all eternity the universe was in God's thought. It did not appear until He spoke. It was His word that was creative.

The Psalmist continues, "By the word of the Lord were the heavens made; and all the host of them by the breath of his mouth" (Psa. 33:6). This explains how it was that Jesus cast out the spirits—not by His thought alone, but by His word. This explains why the authority of the believer is expressed, transmitted, and made effective by the word of testimony. Evil spirits are intelligent, self-conscious personalities who respond to the word of authority. This explains why it is necessary for the believer to speak in the Name of Jesus, and, upon the basis of Calvary's victory, to voice the word of command directly to the afflicting or oppressing evil spirits.

I again encourage you to be specific and to call them by their names, to command them in the Name of Jesus and upon the basis of the shed blood to go back to the abyss and stay there.

To illustrate: I have two boys, David and Jonathan. When I announce, "One of you boys do such and such errand," each looks at the other one and neither one of them goes. I must call one of them by name and speak directly to him before he will go. And he will then probably not do any more than I specifically tell him to do. In order to get results, I must be specific. I cannot get results by speaking in a general way.

The Name High Over All

In the same way, it is necessary to be specific in dealing with Satan and evil spirits. Satan does not care how you talk *about* him. Demons do not fear or flee if you talk *about* them. Authority is transmitted and made effective only when you speak directly to them in the *first person,* always in the Name of Jesus of Nazareth and upon the basis of the shed blood. This, I believe, is the meaning of Revelation 12:11: "They overcame him by the blood of the Lamb, and the word of their testimony." It may not be the exclusive meaning of this passage but I believe that it is the primary meaning.

If you have followed carefully you may now be able to see why this technique is effective. This may explain why it is effective to call demons by their name when seeking to overcome. Since they are self-conscious personalities and have identity, it is necessary to single them out by name. Jesus was specific when He said, "Thou dumb and deaf spirit, . . . come out' (Mark 9:25). It also explains why Jesus asked the demoniac of Gadara, before casting out the demons, "What is thy name?"

People may not realize that demons have names. Paris Reidhead and Carl Tanis, missionaries to Africa, both told me that in Africa demon possession is so common in an aggravated form that the natives actually know the name of the demon that is tormenting them. When we understand that the entire occult world is made up of evil spirits who are intelligent, self-consious personalities, who can feel and will and think, and who therefore have identity, we can better understand why it is necessary to speak directly to them in the first person and identify them by name.

Since Christ has destroyed Satan at the cross

and cancelled all of his rights and claims and since He has delegated the enforcement of Calvary's victory to believers, you can understand why the technique set forth in Revelation 12:11 is effective. Satan will do all he can to frighten and prevent your using these weapons, but when you do use them in full reliance upon Calvary's victory, you will discover for yourselves the power of the blood and the Name of Jesus and the truth of Charles Wesley's hymn:

Jesus, *the name high over all,*
In hell, in earth, and sky!
Angels and men before it fall,
And devils fear and fly."

"These signs shall follow them that believe: In my name shall they cast out devils" (Mark 16:17).

PART TWO

Developing the Personal Prayer Life

The Mystery of Prayer

Besides our little planet, the whole universe was created for one purpose: to provide a suitable habitation for the human race. The human race was created for one purpose: to provide an Eternal Companion for the Son.

After the tragedy of the Fall and God's promise of redemption through His Son, the messianic race was born and nurtured to bring in the Messiah. And the Messiah came for one intent and only one: to give birth to His Church and thus to obtain His Bride.

We see, therefore, that the Church, later to become the Bride of Christ, is the central object and goal not only of history but of all that God has been doing in all realms from all eternity.

In other words, from the very beginning the *one* purpose for the creation of the outer universe is to produce and prepare an Eternal Companion, called the Bride, the Lamb's Wife, for the Son (Rev. 21:9). Because this Bride, the Wife of the Lamb, is to share the throne of the universe as a judicial equal with her divine Lover and Lord following the marriage supper of the Lamb (Rev. 3:21), she must be trained, educated, and prepared for her queenly role.

We are given only glimpses in the Scripture of the duties of the saints in the millenial Kingdom; but it is clear that administration of the great King's will, overseeing of all parts of His vast, eternal realm, will certainly be included. For this unique and distinguished function, God ordained the plan of prayer by which His Bride would enter into personal encounter and conflict with Satan and his hierarchy, overcoming their opposition to God and His kingdom. *This is not to assist God in overcoming him, but to give the Church exercise and practice in overcoming.* Character acquired in overcoming is a necessary prerequisite to rulership with Christ.

Here, I believe, is the sole reason for the method and practice of prayer. It is God's *master plan* to produce overcomers for the throne. Prayer is not to persuade or to assist God except in His training program. It is solely to give the Church exercise and practice in overcoming in order to increase her eternal rank and efficiency. As we learned in Part One in the context of spiritual warfare, prayer is purely, totally and entirely *on-the-job training*. It can be understood in no other context.

The Badge of Rank

I will state it again: God's eternal purpose in the creation of the universe and the human race was to obtain an Eternal Companion for His Son. This fact is part of the mystery revealed in the book of Ephesians and it reaches its illuminative climax in Chapter Five. This chapter expounds the divinely revealed parallel between God's human and divine marriage programs. Verse 32 clarifies the mystery when Paul unequivocally declares that the partners of the marriage program are Christ and His Church. In God's eternal purpose, the Church, as Christ's Eternal Companion, *is to occupy the highest position in the universe short of the Godhead itself.* As the Bride of the Eternal Son, she is to share with Him eternal sovereignty.

Notice these prophecies from the New Testament:

"Don't you know that some day we

Christians are going to judge and govern the world? . . . Don't you realize that we Christians will judge and reward the very angels in heaven?" (1 Cor. 6:2a, 3a, TLB).

"If we suffer, we shall also reign with Him" (2 Tim. 2:12).

"And he that overcometh, and keepeth my works unto the end, to him will I give power [authority] over the nations" (Rev. 2:26).

"To him that overcometh will I grant to sit with me in my throne, even as I also overcame, and am set down with my Father in His throne" (Rev. 3:21).

"And they sang a new song, saying, Thou art worthy to take the scroll, and to open its seals; for thou wast slain and hast redeemed us to God by thy blood out of every kindred, and tongue, and people, and nations; and hast made us unto our God a kingdom of priests, and we shall reign on the earth" (Rev. 5:9, 10, New Scofield).

Redeemed members of the human race, the only race in all creation that was made in the image of God, will constitute this Eternal Companion. Since this companion is to share the throne of the universe with her Lover and Lord, she must be trained, educated, and prepared for her queenly role. Yes, God had something infinitely great in mind when He planned the system of prayer.

On-the-Job Training for Sovereignty

By delegating His authority to her for administering His decisions and enforcing His will upon earth, *God placed the Church in apprenticeship for eternal sovereignty with Christ.* By practicing in her prayer closets the enforcement of heaven's decisions in mundane affairs, the *Church is in on-the-job training for co-sovereignty with Christ over His universal empire.* She must learn the art of spiritual warfare, of overcoming evil forces in preparation for her assumption of the throne.

To enable her to learn the technique of overcoming, God devised the scheme of prayer. To give her on-the-job training, God delegated to her the authority to enforce His will right here on earth. In order to enable her to acquire the character and the "know-how" she will need as co-sovereign, *He has placed upon her the privilege, responsibility, and authority to enforce God's will and administer His decisions in the affairs of earth.*

Notice how often *earth*, her sphere of action, is

emphasized: "Whatsoever thou shalt bind on *earth*"; "Whatsoever thou shalt loose on *earth*"; "If any two of you shall agree on *earth . . .*" (Matt. 16:19, 18:19). This delegation of authority and administrative responsibility for earthly affairs *constitutes the highest honor and elevates her to the highest rank of all created beings.*

God's Original Purpose

It may seem irreverent but is, nevertheless, true that God cannot exalt redeemed humanity any higher in the divine economy without infringing upon the Godhead. While we must understand that infinity separates the Creator from the created, yet from the beginning God planned in Jesus Christ so completely to bridge this gap that redeemed humanity ends up as a full-blooded (generic) member of the family of God, seated with Christ on the throne of the universe as His Bride and Companion. "To him that overcometh will I grant to sit with me in my throne" (Rev. 3:21)

This was no after-thought. It was God's plan from all eternity. "He hath chosen us *in Him* before the foundation of the world" (Eph. 1:4). *This was God's original purpose in the creation of the universe and the human race.* And God's prayer program is His method of preparing the Bride for this supreme rank in His Kingdom.

The Sole Reason for Prayer

May I repeat: I believe the sole reason for the conception, initiation and operation of the system and practice of prayer *is God's master plan to produce overcomers for the throne. Prayer is never to persuade or assist God.* He has bound Himself to the Church's prayers in order to give the Church exercise in overcoming, to increase her eternal rank and efficiency. Therefore, prayer is wholly for the purpose of on-the-job training. *It can be understood in no other context.*

A clear illustration of this is found in Ezekiel 22:30, 31: "And I sought for a man among them, that should make up the hedge, and stand in the gap before me for the land, that I should not destroy it: but I found none. Therefore have I poured out mine indignation upon them; I have consumed them with the fire of my wrath: their own way I have recompensed upon their heads, saith the Lord God."

Why should God seek for a man? Can a man do something that God cannot? Can a man help God except in His training program? The answer is *no.* God ordained the plan of prayer entirely for man's sake. As soon as a person is born again, he enters apprenticeship for rulership in the ages to come. Every born-again believer is a candidate for the highest office in the universe—Bridehood and therefore rulership with Christ. Prayer is God's method of teaching overcoming to candidates for the throne of the universe.

God could have removed Satan by incarcerating him immediately at the moment of his fall, *but He is using him to train His future co-rulers.*

"To him that overcometh will I grant to sit with me in my throne, even as I also overcame; and am set down with my Father in his throne" (Rev. 3:21, 22). This is why Jesus said that He has given believers authority over all the power of the enemy (Luke 10:19).

To many of us, Satan is invincible. Not so. He is only a created being. Learning progressively in time to overcome Satan is the primary qualification for rulership in eternity. This is why God looked for a man to overcome Satan instead of doing it Himself. This also explains why God permits Satan to contest the believer—to give him exercise in overcoming.

Prayer Does Not Influence God

In the past, many have thought that prayer influences God. This is a mistake. *Prayer does not influence God.* God is wholly sovereign. He Himself initiates all prayer that is according to His will. When in His divine wisdom He decides on a course of action in the world He has created and governs, He seeks for a man upon whose heart He can lay a burden, and who will cooperate with Him by voicing God's purpose and desire.

God never answers a prayer which even He

has inspired until He finds a man to verbalize it, at least in his spirit. Our words, our strong desires, our anxieties and tears have no intrinsic power over Satan himself. But because prayer is on-the-job training, words release God's Spirit into action. Because prayer is on-the-job training, it galvanizes heaven into operation. This is why James said, "Ye have not because ye ask not."

Because prayer is on-the-job training it releases the Spirit of God to confront Satan. Only that which originates in heaven has any power against Satan. This is why God does nothing except by prayer and why *prayer is where the action is*. This is the basis of the claim that God regulates the world by prayer. E. M. Bounds said, "God shapes the world by prayer. . . . The prayers of God's saints are the capital stock of heaven by which God carries on His great work upon earth."

An Explanation of Importunity

When God lays a burden of prayer upon you, it is His way of revealing His purpose and will in a particular situation. By this burden God is telling you that He is already mobilizing circumstances to accomplish the purpose of the burden. It is therefore, a substantial encouragement to faith.

If you are convinced that the object represented by your burden is truly of God, since He is all powerful and since He answers all prayer offered in His name, the answer to such a prayer is never in doubt. The only question is your persistence in prayer. If you do not give up, you may be assured that the answer is certain.

I once thought that a burden of prayer meant I was seeking to persuade God to do something He was reluctant to do. Importunity is never to persuade God to do something He has urged you to pray for. The purpose of importunity is to give you exercise in overcoming satanic opposition and to teach you rulership in preparation for the throne. God's purpose in ordaining prayer is not to help Him but to give you training in the exercise of authority over Satan.

When you have learned a new lesson, when you have prayed through to another place of spiritual maturity, then the Holy Spirit is released to bind Satan and the prayer is answered. This is why God seeks for a man, and why Jesus said in Luke 10:19, "Behold, I give unto *you* power [authority] . . . over all the power of the enemy."

Satan's every act, trick, and device is under God's control. He could not move an eyelash without God. He cannot act independently. The reason he is permitted to continue his resistance and opposition is not because God cannot control him; God permits this only so long as it serves His purpose for our growth, development, and maturity.

When we understand that Satan can attack us only with God's permission, and that God's purpose in permitting it is to teach us authority, then we know there is no necessity for our defeat. We know that victory is ours no matter how long and desperate the conflict. We may be assured that as soon as we have learned the new lesson in overcoming, God will take care of Satan.

If the Church Will Not Pray, God Will Not Act

God never goes "over the head" of His Church to enforce His decision. He will not take things out of her hands. To do so would sabotage His training program. Only by bearing this overwhelming weight of responsibility can the Bride be brought to her full stature as co-sovereign of the universe. This is the reason that when she fails, He will wait. This is why He will do nothing in the realm of human redemption until she accepts her responsibility and uses her privilege and prerogative of intercession. *If she will not pray, God will not act, because this would abort His purpose to bring His Church to her full potential as His co-sovereign.*

This was God's plan from the beginning. He will not spoil it now by taking things out of her hands. *He will let the whole world go to destruction first.* His part of the work of redemption is full and complete. But He will not override His

Church. His eternal purpose is the qualifying of His Eternal Companion for entering into full partnership with her Lord in the governing process of the universe. She can be qualified only through the apprenticeship of prayer and intercession. Only thus does she enter into and participate in the eternal purpose of her Lord. *God will do nothing apart from His Church and her prayers.*

The Main Business of the Church

John Wesley said, "God will do nothing but in answer to prayer." S. D. Gordon said that "the greatest thing anyone can do for God and for man is to pray." He also said, "You can do more than pray *after* you have prayed, but you cannot do more than pray *until* you have prayed." This explains his statement, "Prayer is striking the winning blow . . . service is gathering up the result."

E. M. Bounds, who wrote seven books, said, "God shapes the world by prayer. The more praying there is in the world, the better the world will be, the mightier the forces against evil. . . . The prayers of God's saints are the capital stock of heaven by which God carries on His great work upon earth. God conditions the very life and prosperity of His cause on prayer."

If these things are true, then surely *"Prayer should be the main business of our day."*

The Church Holds the Key

Checks used by some business firms require the signatures of two individuals to make them valid. One signature is not enough. Both parties must sign. This illustrates God's method of operating through the prayers and faith of His people. His promises are His checks signed in His own blood. His part was fully completed at Calvary. But because prayer is on-the-job training, no promise is made good until a redeemed man enters the Throne Room of the universe and, by prayer and faith, writes his name beside God's. Then, and not until then, are the check's resources released.

It is like a safety deposit box in the bank vault. The keeper has a key and the owner has a key. Neither key alone will open the box. But when you give the keeper your key, BOTH are inserted and the door flies open, making available all the treasure stored in the box.

Heaven holds the key by which decisions governing earthly affairs are made; but we hold the key by which these decisions are implemented. This being so, then prayer takes on a very different dimension from the conventional notion or understanding. Prayer is not overcoming reluctance in God. It is not persuading Him to do something He is unwilling to do. It is "binding upon earth" that which already has been bound in heaven (Matt. 16:19, Amplified). It is implementing His decision. It is enforcing His will upon earth. Prayer makes possible God's accomplishing what He wants and what He cannot do without it.

The content of all true prayer originates in the heart of God. So it is He who inspires the prayer in the heart of man. The answer to every God-inspired petition is already prepared before the prayer is uttered. When we are convinced of this, then faith for the answer is easy—far easier than it would be otherwise.

Too Busy to Pray

No angel was ever invited to share the high privilege of prayer. No archangel was ever invited into the Throne Room of the universe—only redeemed humanity. And many of us are too busy watching television, following sports, hunting and fishing, bathing and boating, engaging in farming or business, moonlighting. . . . We are so busy with the cares and pleasures of this life, trying to keep up with the trend in new cars, new homes, new appliances, new furniture, that we do not have time to pray.

Someone has described a modern American as a person who drives a bank-financed car over a bond-financed highway on credit-card gas to open a charge acount at a department store so he can fill his Savings-and-Loan financed home with installment-purchased furniture. May this not be also a description of many modern professing Christians? And may not this drive toward materialism be one reason why modern Christians have so little time to pray?

Perhaps some may be thinking: Are we to have nothing at all for ourselves? The answer is, *no.* Christ is to be all and in all. You are not your own. You are bought with a price (1 Cor. 6:19, 20). "And whether therefore ye eat, or drink, or whatsoever ye do, do all to the glory of God" (1 Cor. 10:31).

If you can buy the new car, the new home, the new furniture, the new gadgets, hold down two jobs, etc., for the glory of God—well and good. But think carefully, dear Christian, if we didn't have to have such a high standard of living, would we not have more time to pray? If we were not so intoxicated with travel, pleasure, vacations and recreation, would we not have more time to pray? If we were not so enamored of sports and entertainment, would we not have more time to pray? We have more leisure than ever before—but less time to pray. We are not only cheating God and the world, but we are cheating ourselves.

By our failure to pray, we are frustrating God's high purpose in the ages. We are robbing the world of God's best plan for it, and we are limiting our rank in eternity. *"And I sought for a man among them, . . . but I found none"* (Ezek. 22:30).

The Most Important Activity

"Pray without ceasing" (1 Thess. 5:17). A suggested paraphrase of this passage is: "Make prayer the main business of your life." With few exceptions, through the centuries, the Church has never taken prayer seriously. Few of us take it seriously today. For the most part, prayer has been and still is mostly window dressing, a sort of ritualistic or cosmetic excercise. The Church at large, and most of us individually, use prayer as a salve to our conscience—that is, we pray enough to keep our conscience from barking too loudly.

This is because we do not believe that prayer is where the action is. Let me remind you again of some statements on prayer from great Christian leaders of the past: S. D. Gordon has said that "the greatest thing anyone can do for God and for man is to pray." He has further said that "you can do more than pray *after* you have prayed, but you cannot do more than pray *until* you have prayed." He states that, "Prayer is striking the winning blow . . . service is gathering up the results." John Wesley declared that God does nothing except through prayer.

All of these are astounding statements. There was a time in my life when I considered them mostly "good preacher talk"—that is, the right thing to say; but I had no idea of the theological reasons behind them.

A Spiritual Warfare

The reason is set forth in the 6th chapter of Ephesians, where Paul says, "For our struggle is not against flesh and blood [any physical enemy], but against the rulers, against the authorities, against the powers of this dark world and against the spiritual forces of evil in the heavenly realm" (vs. 12, NIV). This is referring to outer space or the atmosphere surrounding the earth. As C. S. Lovett says, "Evil spirits are just outside your skin."

Evil spirit personalities under the direction of their ruler, the god of this world, swarm the earth in an attempt to foil God's government and control earth's inhabitants; they are constantly inciting them to rebellion against God, against His purposes, aims and plans. The war that began in heaven when Satan was expelled merely changed locations and now continues on earth. All wars, all crime, all violence in the world is incited, is stirred up, by evil spirits operating in the unseen world on the fallen nature of mankind.

Disorder in Human Events

Human events are only a reflection, a projec-

tion, of activities spawned and propagated by satanic armies in the invisible realm. Under the direction of their ruler or prince, the god of this world, these evil spirit personalities flood the earth, seeking to control the government of nations as illustrated in Daniel 10; political activities of occult forces are seen here as the work of actual historic personalities, the prince of Persia and Greece.

The rapid deterioration of morals in the home, the visible organized Church, the State, the Nation and the world are the result of demon activity and influence in philosophy, education, entertainment, religion and politics. In John 10:10, Satan is called "the thief" that comes for one purpose and that is to steal, to kill and destroy. This is the true reason and the only explanation for the strife, disorder and chaos in the social, political and governmental orders.

Sweeping Constitutional Decrees

By God's own decree, this unseen sphere of demon activity, operating in the visible realm of earth, is kept in check because of one fact and one alone. These hordes of intelligent personalities are controlled not by armies, navies, air or police power; they are not subject to guns, bombs, planes or tanks. By God's own choice, in order to train the members of His Bridehood in overcoming, in preparation for eternal rulership with Christ, the only power that controls these invisible principalities and powers is the power of the Holy Spirit released by the prayer and faith of God's holy people. Although all authority in heaven and earth belongs to Christ and Christ alone, *He has now officially vested that authority over Satan in members of His Body, the Church.* "Behold, I give unto you power to tread on serpents and scorpions, and over all the power of the enemy: and nothing shall by any means hurt you" (Luke 10:19).

This was not the first time that the Godhead had delegated authority over Satan. As recorded in Revelation 12, when Satan and his followers were ejected from heaven, it was not the personal intervention of the Godhead that forced him to earth. In that heavenly war, God delegated authority over Satan to Michael and his angels and they became representatives or deputies of the Godhead and sent Satan "like lightning" from the heavenly sphere.

Delegation of Authority

Upon the return of the seventy disciples whom Jesus sent out in evangelism, the authority that was exercised by Michael and his followers was delegated to them. The same power and authority that was previously entrusted to Michael and his hosts was now *officially* vested in the Church. Luke 10:19 quoted above, *is a sweeping, constitutional, governmental decree charged with all of the authority of heaven.* Just as Michael and his forces were one time given authority over Satan and his hierarchy, so now the Church has been designated as God's surrogate, God's deputy on earth.

Although all authority belongs to Christ alone, it now appears that since His ascension and the birth of the Church, He chooses to exercise that authority only and exclusively through the prayer and faith of the Church. This is the only way the Church, His Bride-elect, can be trained, be able to learn overcoming, which is a prerequisite for rulership in the age to come. "To him that overcometh will I grant to sit with me in my throne, even as I also overcame, and am set down with my Father in his throne" (Rev. 3:21).

May I remind you again, because prayer is on-the-job training, Christ, the organic Head, has voluntarily limited the exercise of His authority in earthly affairs to the members of His Body. It belongs to the Bride: She is His hands and feet. She is heaven's enforcement agency.

Because all authority over Satan in earthly affairs has been delegated to His Church, *even Christ himself exercises no authority in mundane affairs except through her prayer and faith.* This is why prayer is where the action is and why prayer should be the main business of the Church. *God does nothing except by prayer.*

Body Politic of the World

Therefore, the praying people are the body politic of the world, and the Church holds the balance of power in world affairs. Not only in future ages is she the ruling and governing force in the social order, but even now—in this present throbbing moment. By means of her prayer power and to the extent to which she uses it, *the praying Church is actually deciding the course of human events.* Some day we shall discover that prayer is the most important factor in shaping the course of human history.

When the books of Heaven are opened and the spiritual history of the nations of the world is unfolded, it will be written for all to read that the "pray-ers"—not the mayors, or kings, or prime ministers, or presidents, or president's men—are the real molders of events.

When the archives of heaven are thrown open for the universe to behold, it will then be revealed that history was made, not in the council chambers of the great, not by armies and navies, not by Parliaments of nations, but in the hidden and secluded prayer closets of the saints. The movements of men and nations of earth are conceived, inspired and motivated in the unseen. The spirit forces in the unseen are monitored, influenced and controlled by the power that is released only by the prayers of God's people. *Verily, the fate of the world is in the hands of nameless saints (Psalms 149:6-9).*

Prayer Is Where the Action Is

Not so many of us possess creative potential. Few of us are blessed with towering personalities, shining gifts, brilliant intellects or golden talents. Because many of us are only ordinary, average, unspectacular persons, we feel that we have been cheated in life. We believe that we are deprived persons of little or no significance.

But the least gifted person who is born again has access to the most creative resource in the entire universe, the resource of prayer. We humans place great stress on the importance of human endowments, including talent, magnetic personality, technique, intellect, cleverness and skill as the principal factors in shaping human events. But God knows that *prayer is where the action is.*

Prayer is the greatest activity anyone can do for God or man. And the least-gifted, the least-endowed, the least-known person in the world, by making prayer the main business of his life, may become greater in God's book than the most highly endowed, the most brilliant and the most famous person in the world who fails to pray.

Untapped Treasures

A brilliant, disciplined mind honed to a razor's edge, a mind impregnated and permeated with all that we associate with the ultimate in intellect, culture, and scholarship, is to be greatly admired and cultivated. We spend years of study, labor, and toil to acquire these disciplines. But there is something more supremely important and fundamental.

There is a vast store of spiritual wisdom, insight and understanding which can never be tapped by the intellect alone. In Colossians 2:3 Paul insists that "all the treasures of wisdom and knowledge" are hidden, that is, kept secret in Christ. It is impossible to exploit fully the spiritual advantage of academic knowledge without access to the "treasures of wisdom and knowledge" that are hidden in Christ. The spirit makes those treasures available mainly through our devotional life, in the time spent alone with God.

A few hours alone with God can open up treasures of wisdom and knowledge in Christ which may have eluded one during years of purely academic training. Christ is the original source of all knowledge. One may learn much about Christ and spiritual things from the written and recorded works of others, but that is "second-hand" knowledge, which is not to be despised. But if one is willing to spend time alone with God and make prayer the main business of his life, he may tap the original source of all wisdom and knowledge for himself.

All original wisdom comes only by revelation of the Holy Spirit from God himself. Only the truth that comes to one from God himself is original, and it is this truth alone that imparts authority to any ministry. Therefore, *the most excellent academic training is no substitute for a deep devotional life.*

Preach or Pray?

It is suggested that the Apostle Paul may have done more for his churches by his prayers than by his writings. Be that as it may, it is probable that many of us may do more for our people by our praying than by our preaching, no matter how academically excellent it may be.

We spend years studying subjects like Church History, Homiletics, Hermeneutics, Sermon Building, Theology, English and others. All of these may be helpful. But if we come out of seminary without learning to pray, without learning that prayer is striking the winning blow and service is gathering up the results—if we come out of seminary without learning that prayer is the most important thing anyone can do for God or man, and without making prayer the main business of our lives—then no matter how fluent, eloquent or articulate we may be, we are poorly equipped for our task.

"Our fight is not against any physical enemy: it is against organizations and powers that are spiritual. We are up against the unseen power that controls this dark world, and spiritual agents from the very headquarters of evil." (Eph. 6:12, Phillips). The only power that is effective in this realm is the power of the Holy Spirit and by His own choice, that power is liberated and released *only by the prayer and faith of praying people.* This is why Harold O'Chester said, "Don't initiate more than you can saturate with prayer."

You may learn much by diligent study. You may learn much in the classroom. You may be edified by hearing sermons and lectures and by listening to television and teaching tapes, but God's deepest secrets are reserved for those who take time to wait upon the Lord, who take time to be alone with Him. He has many secrets, many spiritual visions, many hidden revelations and insights which will be shared only in long hours of waiting upon God in the secret place of prayer. If we begrudge the time spent alone with God, if we will not wait upon Him, we must be content to remain spiritually naive, inexperienced and immature.

If we will not take time to be alone with God, we forfeit the most priceless and invaluable secrets known to divine intelligence. God waits to share "the treasures of wisdom and knowledge" with those who take time to listen. In our devotional life, time is of essence. *If we do not take time to pray, our devotional life will be defective, anemic and weak.*

Satan's Most Successful Strategy

Satan's most successful strategy to dilute a ministry is to keep God's minister so occupied with reading the latest bestsellers, organizing evangelistic campaigns, studying successful methods of church growth, keeping so busy in administration, visitation, social service, sports activities, counseling, putting out fires of opposition and criticism, that his devotional life is starved.

Activism has its place, but the place is after prayer. As Gordon said, "You can do more than pray after you have prayed, but you cannot do more than pray until you have prayed."

Few of us really believe in our hearts that prayer is where the action is. Many of us are convinced that a brilliant, polished intellect is where the action is; that scholarship, faultless logic and reasoning is where the action is; that psychology is where the action is; that fluency of thought and speech is where the action is; that stentorian rhetoric and articulateness is really where the action is. Others believe that a magnetic personality or that organizational ability, administrative and managerial expertise, business acumen, social service and community leadership—all of these are really where the action is.

I make no effort to discredit any of these; all may be profitable and contribute to the success of a ministry. Maclaren says that if God cannot use our wisdom, He can use our ignorance less. But in the warfare against evil spirit personalities with whom we are engaged, one thing and one alone is effective—the supernatural power of the Holy Spirit that is put into practice only by believing prayer. I quote again from S. D. Gordon: "Prayer is striking the winning blow. Service is gathering up the results."

Harold O'Chester has a host of brothers and sisters, who, like him, came out of school thinking that their success depended upon their cleverness, their ability to perform, their education, their gimmicks or motivational ability—never on the supernatural. He says that we train and teach people to do everything but the one business that will pay the most dividends—*time alone with God in prevailing, intercessory prayer.*

PART THREE

Turning on the Switch

You Have Healing Already

If you are truly born again and have Christ dwelling within you, you already have healing within you, *for healing is in Christ*. You could not receive the Saviour without also receiving the Healer, for they are both the same Person. You do not receive the Saviour at one time and the Healer at another time.

When you received Christ, you did not receive Him in installments but in His entirety. And the Word says, "I am the Lord that healeth thee" (Ex. 15:26). The tense used is continuous present. Isaiah 53:5 teaches that if we have Christ, we are already healed: "By his stripes we are healed." Therefore, although you may be even now suffering with pain or other symptoms or appearances of sickness, if you have Christ within, you are already healed— that is, you have within you the Source of all life and health. "In him was life" (John 1:4), meaning that Christ is the very source and author of every kind of life. If life is in Christ, if healing is in Christ, if Christ be within you, then life and healing are already within you.

Realization

Although the life is there, although the health is there, it will do you no good if you do not realize that it is there, if you have little or no consciousness of its presence within you. If someone were to place one thousand dollars on deposit for you, it would do you no good until you were convinced that it was there for you, that it was in reality yours. It could be there and be legally yours but it would be of no benefit to you if you were not conscious or convinced that it was yours. No matter by what right it is yours, it would still be of no value to you until you were fully conscious of its presence there.

Many a man has been rich who did not know it. Many a man has lived in poverty, eking out a meager existence upon a barren ranch on the western plains while underneath lay rich deposits of oil, but which were only later discovered. Of such it could be truly said, "Although you live in poverty, nevertheless you are rich—and you do not know it." And of every real saint it truly can be said, "Although you may be suffering, you are nevertheless healed; you are well and don't know it. And you will *feel* well when you become thoroughly convinced that you *are* well because you have health and everything else you need when you receive Christ."

Your relief from all symptoms of illness only awaits your full and complete realization of a fact which already exists. The disappearance of all physical evidences of disease will keep pace with the development of a clear consciousness of the presence of this healing power within you now. This is only another way of saying, "According to your faith, be it unto you" (Matt. 9:29). Thus you see that the whole problem of the removal of symptoms is the problem of fully developing the consciousness of this healing power which is already yours.

Keep the Way Clear

Anything which dims the consciousness of the presence of Christ within is sure to hold back your deliverance. One least thing with which the Spirit of God has a controversy in one's life is sufficient to dim the consciousness of His presence and delay the blessing.

You must remember that the foremost purpose and primary result of Christ's life within you is ethical and moral and that anything which hinders the purifying work of this life in the moral nature of man hinders its healing work in his physical body. Any cult or system of healing which ignores or fails to emphasize the necessity of careful spiritual adjustment is open to suspicion.

Here is the distinguishing mark between true biblical healing and healing known as metaphysical healing. Metaphysical healing, healing taught by false cults, lays little or no stress upon the necessity for moral and spiritual adjustments, the surrender of sin, of the world and worldly amusements, practices and associations. Biblical healing is intensely spiritual and ethical and emphasizes the necessity of death to self, sin and things of earth. Any known sin, any rejected light, any lack of spiritual adjustment will dim the consciousness of the presence of Christ within and hinder your deliverance.

Building a Clear Consciousness

When Christ is there and the consciousness of His presence is clear, the next step is to build a clear consciousness, to build conviction of the fact that healing is already yours. And that is faith. Faith is "the evidence of things not seen" (Heb. 11:1). Mind you, that although the "things" spoken of are not seen, they nevertheless do exist and faith is only becoming convinced that they do exist.

I used to think that faith was believing that something was true which was not true and that such believing would make the thing come true. Nothing could be more absurd. God never asks us to believe that something is true if it is not. God never asks us to believe a lie nor teaches that believing a lie will make it true. Faith is not telling or acting a pious lie. Believing that something is true which is not true will never make it true.

Faith is the acceptance of a fact which already exists but which has not yet been manifested to the senses. That is what Paul meant when he said that faith is the evidence or conviction or consciousness of things not seen.

Electricity in the Wires

To illustrate: in the building where you are sitting, there are many wires and cables that are full of electricity; but you do not see it nor experience any manifestation of it until you turn on the switch. It would be difficult to explain to people who have had no experience with electricity that electric current is even now throbbing in the wires within the walls. Until the switch is turned on it is not visible, but it is there and you know it is there. That is faith in the unseen—a conviction of a fact which exists but which has not yet been manifested to the senses.

When you are born again, you are "wired up," connected with the dynamo of resurrection life which first manifests itself in the spiritual or unseen realm. Just as turning an electric switch sends electric current, which is already within the building, flowing through the light bulb and banishing darkness, so faith, which is turning on the switch—making the contact that sends resurrection power, which is already within you, flowing into your body and banishing symptoms of disease.

Positive Contact

In order to get results in the electrical field it is necessary to have a good contact. You do not have to take out a foot of the wire in order to break the contact and stop the flow of power. A very small bit of corrosion or a thin piece of paper between the switchpoints is sufficient. When your automobile lights have failed or your motor has refused to start, you have sometimes discovered that the reason was corroded battery posts. The battery was throbbing with power but the machine was totally disabled by an almost imperceptible film of corrosion. In the realm of divine healing, it is just as necessary to have a good contact. In fact, that is the whole problem. Very small, almost imperceptible acts of self-will are often sufficient to break the spiritual circuit and stop the flow of power from its hidden source within, to the body cells or circuit. The slightest reservation or an unforgiving spirit may make it impossible for you to develop the clear, vital conviction or unwavering faith without which, James tells us, we may expect nothing from the Lord (James 1:6, 7). *A positive contact is necessary.*

Switching on the Power

When you know you are born again; when you are sure that you are walking in all the light; when there is nothing to dim the consciousness of the abiding presence of Christ within you; when you are thoroughly convinced that that Presence is a healing Presence and the Antagonist and Conqueror of all disease—then you are ready to "switch on the power." And this is very simple. You do it by speaking your "word of faith," by claiming or affirming that which is already a fact.

As we said before, <u>faith is not believing something that is not true. It is not telling a pious lie. It is the acceptance of a fact which already exists in reality but which has not yet been manifested</u> to the senses. "Faith is the evidence of things not seen"—things which nevertheless exist in reality. Faith sees and accepts the fact as true, turns on the switch by the spoken word—that is, acting upon the reliability of the fact, and witnesses the manifestation of the fact.

The order is: Fact, faith and then feeling. Realize the fact first, increase your realization of the fact by speaking or declaring it, and then you will feel it in your body. You turn on the switch by affirmation or declaration.

Turn a promise of healing into an affirmation and keep declaring it until you are fully convinced of its reality, until you believe it in your heart without wavering; and you will see that your symptoms will disappear. There is power in the spoken word to clarify and strengthen faith. You discovered long ago that every time you testify to some spiritual experience, that experience is strengthened. Speaking your word of faith, audibly declaring the truth of the fact, will strengthen your faith *in that fact*; it will make the truth so clear and real to your consciousness that a positive contact will be made through which the resurrection power, although unseen but abiding within you, will become manifest in your body.

Strengthening the Contact

You have heard of men who have told an untruth so often that they came to believe it themselves. If a man, by the spoken word, can convince himself of the truth of a lie, why cannot you and I, by the spoken word, convince ourselves of the truth of a fact which has its basis in the unfailing Word and promise of God?

Jesus said, "I am the vine, ye are the branches" (John 15:5). We know that the life that is in the vine is likewise in the branches. Therefore every truly born-again child of God has a perfect scriptural right to say, notwithstanding contrary symptoms, "Because I am a branch of the true Vine, therefore Thy life is my life; and I am made perfectly whole."

Paul says in 1 Corinthians 6:15, "Know ye not that your bodies are the members of Christ?" and in Ephesians 5:30, "For we are members of his body, of his flesh, and of his bones." Therefore every true believer has a scriptural right to say, "Because I am a member of Thy body, therefore Thy life is my life; and I am constantly, gloriously healed."

Repeat such affirmations aloud many times a day. Spend five or ten or fifteen minutes a day affirming aloud these declarations, and you will find that they are true and that His resurrection life will be manifested in your mortal body. Your symptoms will pass away. They will vanish in direct proportion to the clarity and strength of your faith. The moment your faith is perfect, that moment you will be completely delivered. "According to your faith, be it unto you."

Many people have hesitated to say that they were healed before their symptoms disappeared because they feared that they might be telling a lie. By recognizing that healing is in Christ and Christ is within you, you need have no fear of boldly declaring that you are healed, because you have the source of life and health within.

I have only been endeavoring to show you how to develop a perfect faith. Follow these directions literally and you will get results. Praise God!

God's Word Is Reliable

Perhaps you are still wondering how you can say that you are healed when the symptoms still remain. Although, to all appearances, the sun travels around the earth, yet because the writer of your geography says that instead the earth rotates toward the sun, you utterly ignore the testimony of your senses and accept the word of the geographer.

Do you remember how skeptical you were when you first read that the sun did not actually travel around the earth every twenty-four hours? And yet you now accept this word and boldly declare that it is true although even yet, to all appearances, the sun does circle the earth.

Will you refuse to place as much confidence in God's Word as you do in the geographer? When God says, "I am the Lord that healeth thee," accept it just like you do the word of the geographer. Ignore the symptoms which are appearances only; believe the reality which is Christ's life within you; turn on the switch by affirmation, declaration, testimony and praise; and you can prove for youself that *the healing power that is already within will manifest itself in your body.*

PART FOUR

Spiritual Warfare

Our Own Lives
by Mrs. Paul E. Billheimer

Paul E. Billheimer was born in the home of a circuit pastor before the turn of the century, the middle one of nine children. He was nurtured in an atmosphere of prayer and implicit faith in the inerrancy of the Word of God. He was gloriously born again at the age of fourteen and maintained that relationship by a diligent devotional and prayer life. His public ministry began at age sixteen when his father's failing health necessitated his assistance.

His college work was interrupted by World War I and the Fifth Infantry Officer's Training School from which he was graduated. Following discharge from the service, he attended Houghton

101

College, Taylor University, and was graduated
from Marion College in 1923.

Although God had called him to the ministry
of the Word, his months in the military had
brought him in touch with a world of personal
ambitions which was new and foreign to him. In-
triguingly unobtrusive and ever so insidious, it
made its imprint in his thinking. Gradually his
own ambitions began to embrace far-flung fields
of intellectual excellence and exploration which
would eventually lead him far from the simple
ministry of the Word.

Upon graduation from college, he accepted an
invitation to teach in a Christian junior college in
a univeristy city where he could also begin his
graduate study. When the fall semester had
scarcely begun, he found himself in a total physical collapse with a far-advanced case of tuberculosis of the lungs, abdomen, and lower bowel.
There was little or no hope for recovery from a
medical viewpoint.

This was probably one of the darkest days of
Mr. Billheimer's life. But it was the beginning of a
tremendous training program which God was in-
stituting to bring him into a life-long ministry,
not only of the Word itself but also a ministry in
spiritual warfare. This message would eventually
reach around the world through his books, especially through the prayer message of *Destined for
the Throne*.

Not only does God have a blueprint and long-range plans for our lives, but Satan and his hierarchy also have long-range plans which endeavor to defeat God's plans. A fierce spiritual warfare results. Few of us are aware of this "pitched battle" that goes on in the unseen world continually.

In the days of Mr. Billheimer's illness, we were almost totally untaught along these lines. And also at that time, there was very little teaching on divine healing as a privilege and provision for every child of God. We knew that God could heal and we knew that He sometimes did. However, we were under the impression that one must first have a special revelation from God that it was His will to heal in this particular case. As a result, we lived through 3½ long, dark, discouraging, and almost hopeless years. A few people, a mere handful, held on to their faith that God would heal Mr. Billheimer and send us out into the ministry again. One of those was his mother who often said, "Paul, I believe I will live to hear you preach again." Mrs. Billheimer, although also untaught along these lines, never gave up hope that he would be healed.

On the evening of January 27, 1927, Mr. Billheimer read the testimony of a man who had been healed and given a few more years of soul winning. As he meditated upon the testimony, a tremendous desire to have at least a few sheaves to lay at the Master's feet began to stir within him.

For the first time since his ambitions had veered off course, a deep willingness, even a great longing, to preach the gospel possessed him. He began to pray, "Lord, if You will heal me, I will give *all* of my life and strength to the ministry of the Word."

Here is his own testimony of that time: "About four o'clock on the morning of January 28, 1927, I was awakened. I was not aware that the Lord had awakened me but 'ere long I discerned His glorious Presence. At once I thought, 'God must be wanting to heal me.' Then as I basked in this glorious consciousness of His presence, I thought, 'If He is wanting to heal me, *why not now?*' I continued to commune with Him and within a short time, maybe five minutes, I had covenanted with Him as my *healer.* For several hours I communed with Him, thanking Him for my healing and offering Him the worship and adoration of my being. It was a never-to-be-forgotten experience of His presence.

"But when rising time arrived, my symptoms remained the same, I still was in great pain and weakness. You see, I was in the most serious condition of all of the 3½ years. According to two specialists, I was at death's door. They said I only had a few days, or weeks at the most, to live. New areas of the disease were breaking out in my lungs, old scars were breaking down, the tubercular peritonitis was active and very painful. The tubercular ulcers in my lower bowel were very actively discharging large amounts of blood and pus every day. None of these conditions appeared to be changed but I had a deep inner witness that 'my 400 years without a vision' had ended and *I was healed!*

"It was several days before I had the courage to tell anyone. I first ventured to confide it to my mother who rejoiced with me and encouraged my faith. Next, I ventured to confide it to Mrs. Billheimer who rallied behind me and gave me all of the support she knew how. In about two weeks I had gained sufficient strength to dress, put on heavy wraps and walk out to the end of our small lot and back in the February snow and cold of an Indiana winter.

"Each day I walked a little farther, and soon I was walking several city blocks. Each day brought new exhilaration of spirit and a strengthening of my faith. A revival began at our local church and I ventured to attend. Our friends rejoiced and praised the Lord with us. Then came the *big* test. The evangelist, whom I had known all of my life, asked me to preach on Saturday evening. This was only *four weeks* after my healing from my 'death bed.' I was terrified. I was afraid that my illness would return if I refused to preach and I didn't know what awful emergency might erupt if I exercised my lungs to that extent. It was the most colossal step of faith I had ever taken when I said, 'I'll try.'

"Saturday evening came and I was in the pulpit. I rose to speak at 8 o'clock, and when I came to myself again, the clock said nine o'clock! For one solid hour I had poured out my soul with as much vigor and intensity as I was capable of, and I felt no ill effect. When I wakened Sunday morning I was feeling much stronger and better than at any time. I attended the morning worship service and gave public testimony to my amazing improvement. I made the statement that 'The Lord has done so much for me and my improvement is so great that now *I know* I am healed, no matter what happens.'

 "I did not know it, but *this was a tragic mistake.* I placed my faith in the disappearance of symptoms instead of the Word of God. I had unwittingly opened the door wide for my first fierce encounter in spiritual warfare for my healing. I do not have words adequately to describe the fierce battle that set in some time before midnight that Sunday night and raged for possibly 24 to 36 hours. Every symptom which I had suffered during that long 3½ years returned in intensified form during that terrible night of suffering and spiritual conflict.

Finally, the Lord was able to get through to my consciousness that my faith must rest upon His Word alone. As soon as I returned to that solid foundation, the symptoms began to disappear and my restoration continued at a miraculous pace. In a few weeks I was giving my testimony every Sunday in one of the churches of our district, and by August I had officially returned to a pastorate."

This testimony is the background for an intensive ministry of nearly 55 years. This includes the pastorate, twenty years of radio ministry, Christian education as well as writing, and, now, television.

"Following my healing," Mr. Billheimer continues, "my message immediately broadened to include Christ for the body as well as for our salvation. My theme soon became *'Christ for soul and body.'* When the time came that I wrote the story of my healing, that was the title given the little book. As a result of my emphasis on Christ for *all* our needs, many marvelous healings began to take place among those whose faith was inspired both by my own testimony as well as by my preaching of the Word."

In June of 1936 the Lord led us to take what, to us, was a tremendous step of faith and open an independent ministry in the city of Anderson, Indiana. In reality it was a totally *dependent* ministry for we were in total dependence upon the Lord for *everything*. Our total assets consisted of an old car, a homemade trailer house, a tent top, three children and the Word of God. We had signed a contract with the local radio station for one hour Sunday morning. This time must be paid for in advance. Our purse was empty.

We pulled our little trailer onto a vacant lot on West 2nd St. and pitched the tent top under the tall trees on the front of the lot. We borrowed a few benches and some sidewalls for the tent and held our first service on the evening of our 16th wedding anniversary, June 15, 1936. A handful of adults and a larger group of children were present, totaling 27 in our audience.

We continued to worship in the tent until well into the month of October. September was especially cold and wet and we were sorely tested. Housing was almost an impossible item at that time, but—in answer to prayer and all in one week—we moved into a large, four-bedroom house which gave room for our family, a study for Mr. Billheimer and ample office space. And at that same time, we also moved our services into an old building as a Tabernacle. It had been a machine shop of some sort and certainly needed much cleaning. We quipped to our radio friends that we had stained glass windows and the stain could not be removed.

From this most humble beginning, God did a precious work during the next twenty years. We began to learn in an ever-expanding depth and breadth the importance of spiritual warfare. In many and varied ways we learned increasingly that "we wrestle not against flesh and blood, but against principalities, against powers, against the rulers of the darkness of this world, against spiritual wickedness in high places."

After the first year we were constantly in a building program of one kind and another. First there was the Tabernacle, then Faith Hall, the combination office, dormitory, and classroom building. All of this was necessitated by the growing radio ministry, the increasing local congregation, and the need for Bible classes in the form of a night school. Eventually there developed a full-time Bible Institute, a Christian high school which later became state accredited, and, last of all, a Christian day school. As the school began to take form, an adequate campus became a necessity.

It seemed that pressing needs and a perpetually exhausted treasury kept us in a constant prayer battle, a distinct *prayer warfare.* As we acquired a wooded area to develop as a campus, we not only had to pray in funds but all kinds of building permits, annexation to the city in order to receive both water and sewer service, fire protection and all of the things that are inherent in a large building program. By this time we had built our own radio station operating under the direction of the school, and there were all kinds of needs to be prayed in for that department of the ministry. We had felt led of the Lord to operate on a pay-as-you-go basis.

In the beginning of the ministry under the little tent on 2nd Street, a morning prayer group was formed which continued to operate for at least 25 years. It was the very "backbone" of the work. A group of faithful prayer warriors met every morning, Monday through Friday, in the specified Prayer Room to pray for the multitudes of prayer requests from our radio listeners, the financial needs of the work, but most of all, for the spiritual needs of all concerned. This included the leadership and the office staff plus laborers of all kinds who were working on the various building projects.

Very early in the work, Friday was set aside for fasting and prayer at the noon hour. This was entirely voluntary but practically all of our staff joined in this noon fasting-prayer service. Even after the school was in operation many of the High School students and more of the Bible Institute students chose to join this Friday noon prayer service. Lunch was always provided in the dining room for those who did not choose to fast. We were often amazed at how many teenagers chose to fast and pray. It was not uncommon for Bible Institute students to fast for several days at a time. God moved in remarkable ways as people of all ages really prayed and bound the forces of darkness and prevailed in the might of His power.

The great missionary challenge of Kipling's, "Something more! Something lost behind the

Ranges! Go and find them!" seemed to embody the urge that drove my husband on. No sooner did he reach the top of one "peak" until a greater and higher one loomed before him. A relentless burden to reach the masses gave him no rest.

While his ministry was always of an evangelistic character, seeking to reach the unsaved with the gospel, his paramount burden was for the growth and maturity of the believer. The Lord seemed to always lead him into new and deeper areas of study. These were a constant challenge to the believers in his audience, whether a local congregation of which he was the pastor or those in his radio audience.

When television rocketed into popularity and every residential area of our cities became veritable forests of TV antennae, he immediately saw them as a ready-made mission field. Many people responded to this vision and shared his concern. However, many spiritual people were, at that time, strongly opposed to believers having a television receiver in their homes because of the character of most programming. But the vision and the burden to implement it with a Christian television station persisted, and in 1957 the station was built and was on the air with an excellent test pattern ready for programming.

Then without warning the Lord permitted Mr. Billheimer's energies to collapse. At that time we supposed that a few months away from the campus and rest from responsibilities would restore us both so that we could return and continue to assist in the ministry with someone else carrying the administrative load.

Concerning God's own plan for our future, 1 Corinthians 2:9 expresses it best: "Eye hath not seen, nor ear heard, neither have entered into the heart of man, the things which God hath prepared for them that love him." Our wildest flight of imagination could never have envisioned the next twenty years, much less these five that have followed.

The years of rest which we envisioned when we drove away from the campus that day in August of 1957 stretched into twenty long, heartbreaking years of sorrow and disappointment. I have often wondered about Moses' thoughts as he cared for Jethro's sheep at the backside of the desert near Horeb those forty long years when he had no word from his people in Egypt. He did not forget the careful instruction and teaching which his mother instilled into him during the years that she acted as nursemaid for Pharaoh's daughter's adopted son whom she pulled out of the little basket in the reeds and rushes. How well he remembered that God had promised His people a deliverer. Jochabed had told her son again and again that he was "no ordinary child" (Heb. 11:23, NIV). He must have remembered often how greatly his people had misunderstood his motive when he had tried to help them. What a trememdous heartbreak those forty years must have been to Moses—until the day he saw the bush aflame! But it was no ordinary fire; the bush was not consumed.

Our "burning bush" day came in the night hours of the first week of August, 1976, when my husband was walking the floor of our little cabin home in the large, undeveloped woods just outside Atlanta, Georgia. He was travailing in prayer on my behalf. Two and a half years previously I had suffered a severe heart attack which was diagnosed as congestive heart failure with severe angina. Since that time I had been in and out of the hospital many times and was at that time in total bed rest at home. The cardiologist had warned him months before to be prepared for anything. He said I was liable to have a fatal attack at any time. My doctor who was an internist had told me during my recent hospitalization that he did not expect my heart ever to get better. And now I was on total bed rest at home. My husband felt that he had his back to the wall.

Both of us were under great pressure from the enemy. For nearly fifty years the Lord had healed us, our children, and scores and scores of people under my husband's ministry. *Why* were we unable to touch the Lord by faith for deliverance for both of us now? We were at our extremity. God often has to get His children in that place in order to do His best work in them.

As he prayed that night, my husband finally heard a very "still, small voice" speaking deeply within his spirit. It said, "I shall not die, but live, and declare the works of the Lord" (Psalm 118:17).

"But," my husband argued, "that is the Word that You gave me for my healing almost fifty years ago." As he continued to ask the Lord for a word for me, the Lord again repeated the first experience. When this same Word came to him the third time, he finally began to realize that the Lord was quickening the very same Scripture to him for *my* restoration which He had given him for his own healing from tuberculosis almost fifty years previously. His faith began to rise—but feebly at first.

During the next two nights the Lord continued to quicken the Word to him. One time it was from Jeremiah 30:17, "For I will *restore* health unto thee, and I will heal thee of thy wounds, saith the Lord." As his own faith became stronger, he came to my room and shared with me the things the Lord had given to him. My own spirits were very low but I was constantly crying out to the Lord for a Word on which to pin my faith.

You see, neither of us had ever felt that my husband's mininstry was finished. It had merely stopped abruptly without being finished. Since my special calling from the Lord was the "backside of my husband's ministry, to support and encourage him," then my ministry was not finished either. This deep, inner consciousness kept both of us fighting this seemingly interminable battle for life itself. But not a glimmer of light was piercing the darkness of our "valley of the shadow of death."

When my husband shared Jeremiah 30:17 with me, my faith leaped to grasp the word *restore*. The Spirit seemed to give that expression to me: "*I will restore health to thee.*" I began to lay hold with hope again and my faith grew and expanded. In a few days my strength had increased and slowly, agonizingly slowly, I began to take a few steps.

Speaking of warfare—this was warfare of the fiercest kind. Only those who have passed through a *long*, fierce siege of spiritual warfare can understand the agony of spirit that such experiences bring.

That was five years ago, and the joy and rejoicing now far more than repay the sufferings of the battles. In perhaps ten days I was able to walk to the living room without adverse heart reactions and my strength was gradually returning. Within three weeks I was able to sit in the recliner chair all day and answer the telephone which sat beside my chair.

At this point I must pick up the thread from another viewpoint. About a year and a half previous to this time, on March 7, 1975, our little book *Destined for the Throne* had come off the press and the first copies had reached us. That message was born in the prayer closet. It had been developed through much soul travail, and now the matter of its circulation was our chief burden.

We were doing all that we knew how to assist CLC, our publisher, to get it before the Christian reading public. It was being distributed in many areas in the Eastern half of the nation but, so far, we had not heard a single word from the West Coast. For many weeks, perhaps a few months, it had been a special item in our family prayers each morning. We were asking the Lord to give us an outlet on the West Coast.

Just how wonderfully He was working, we did not know. We may never know just how a woman, an interior decorator, got a copy of *Destined for the Throne*. The book evidently meant something to her, because she left a copy for Jan and Paul Crouch one day when she was doing some work in their house.

It was early in August, at the time that the Lord was giving my husband Scripture to stimulate our faith for my recovery from the "hopeless" heart condition, that Jan found this copy of *Destined for the Throne* and began to read it. When Paul came home, she said, "Honey, here is a book you *must* read. It is exactly what we need right now."

They, too, were passing through a fierce battle with the enemy concerning the work of Trinity Broadcasting Network. They began to read to each other by turns until they finished the book. Paul got copies for the staff and required everyone to read it. They all began to pray in a different way. The prayer message of *Destined for the Throne* was beginning to get through to many of them, but especially to Paul and Jan. God began to move in special ways and, in Jan's own words, "Things began to turn around for TBN, and a whole new day began to dawn." Paul gave a copy of the book to the director of a special convention, Jerry Barnard, and suggested that he "get that man to speak in your conference on the Holy Spirit in January." Jerry read the book and decided to do just that.

On August 25, 1976, as I sat in my recliner chair there in the little old cabin in the woods outside Atlanta, Georgia, the phone rang. A voice said, "This is Gil Jones, and I am calling for Christian Faith Center in San Diego, California. We are laying plans for our annual Conference on the Holy Spirit which is held in January. Our pastor, Jerry Barnard, has read your book, *Destined for the Throne,* and he would like for Mr. Billheimer to come for a daily seminar on the book during our conference in January."

This invitation was like a bombshell hitting our little cabin. A daily seminar in San Diego,

California, when we had been shut away from the active Christian public for most of twenty years?

But we were even more stunned when, in about two hours, we received another long-distance call, this time from Titusville, Florida, with a similar message. A Southern Baptist pastor had read *Destined for the Throne,* and he wanted my husband to come soon for a series of meetings giving the prayer message of the book.

God must be moving to do something new, not only *for* us but also *through* us, we thought. The Spirit within us let us know that we *had* to respond to these invitations.

After much praying and several telephone calls, arrangements were finally made for us to go to San Diego in January. This was the first indication we had that *Destined for the Throne* was being read on the West Coast.

A few days later, when talking by phone to our Publisher, he said, "You will be interested to know that we have just shipped 10,000 copies of *Destined* to the West Coast." My question was, "where?" He thought it was some broadcasting station, but he did not remember the name.

We learned later that it was Trinity Broadcasting Network, but we had never heard of them. Was it a radio or television network? Who were they to be that interested in *Destined for the Throne*?

When plans were finalized for us to go to San

Diego, we wrote to TBN saying that we planned to visit some friends in Santa Ana at the end of January and we would be interested in visiting TBN and meeting the people who were so interested in our book that they ordered 10,000 copies. We received a call right back from the office asking if we would be guests on their Praise The Lord program on Tuesday evening, February 1.

We were happy to accept, and that night turned out to be a memorable, never-to-be-forgotten night. Once that interview started, it was hard to know who was more excited, Paul F. Crouch or Paul E. Billheimer. Suffice it to say that on Tuesday night, February 1, 1977, the Praise the Lord program continued straight through to 1 a.m. instead of signing off at the usual 11 p.m. or 11:30 p.m. During this interview, Paul asked my husband right on camera if he would be interested in a Bible teaching series on TBN. I knew instantly that my husband would never sleep one wink the remainder of that night. He didn't.

The next day a taping schedule was arranged, and soon we were at work putting *Destined for the Throne* on video tape to be aired five days a week over Channel 40, covering Southern California.

What was God doing? Was He beginning to bring into being the fulfillment of the shattered vision of twenty years ago? Was a television ministry opening before our very eyes? The Psalmist describes us, "We were like them that dream."

While we were making the set of tapes, Paul and Jan kept suggesting that we move to California and take a place on their Bible teaching staff. My husband was 80 years of age and I was 75. Such a move seemed preposterous and yet—. God had already done the impossible and for what purpose was He restoring my heart? I, who at the first of August could not walk ten feet without a violent heart reaction, was now able to walk from one part of the long building to another, sit at a desk and assist in taping programs for hours a day. Was this the way God planned for my husband to "finish his ministry"?

Finally, we felt at peace to accept the invitation, and in April of 1977 we returned to Georgia and sold what little "junk" we had left. (We soon learned that we had had it so long it was now in the antique class and worth money. Were we ever surprised!)

On May 3, we arrived back in Southern California and "made a new nest" in an apartment near TBN. We then began the task of becoming a real part of Trinity Broadcasting Network. It was *spiritual warfare* that brought us to TBN, and it is continued spiritual warfare that keeps us here and makes this ministry *our* ministry.

We firmly believe that *prayer is where the action is.*

A FINAL WORD

A Call to Prayer Warfare

Trinity Broadcasting Network was born in an agony of prayer and intercession. Every step has been taken over the intense opposition of Satan and all hell. Every advance has been the result of prayer warfare at a cost of blood, sweat, tears, and paeans of praise. As a symbol of TBN's utter dependence upon God, its total dedication to prayer warfare, and its faith in the supernatural, a seven-foot prayer clock stands in Studio C. In the time slots surrounding the clock are many thousands of names of prayer warriors who have pledged to give a specified period in prayer at a designated time for TBN and God's cause in general every day. When the Billheimers joined the teaching staff on TBN, President Paul Crouch appointed them as *Keepers of the Prayer Clock.*

121

Each one who pledges to pray receives a certificate bearing his signature. The Billheimers are seeking the cooperation of *one million prayer warriors.*

When the World Missions Building was erected, a beautiful prayer tower graced the center front and was named the *Destined for the Throne* Prayer Tower. Its purpose is to convey to the church that *prayer is where the action is* and should be *the main business of the church.*

Today the church in South Korea is the best demonstration of this truth that we know. More than any other nation, South Korea has caught the vision of the effectiveness of prayer warfare. In no other country has the church so fully proved that *prayer is where the action is.* In no other nation in the world is the church making *prayer the main business of her life* as in the South Korean church. In a dimension totally foreign to ease-loving America, or to any other nation, Korean believers have made prayer their highest priority. It is known that all over South Korea thousands upon thousands frequently gather to pray all night.

The Prayer Mountain near Seoul, Korea is occupied continuously by hundreds upon hundreds of believers who are giving days and nights to fasting and prayer. God is using the church in South Korea to spearhed the worldwide revival which heralds His imminent return. It is said that the church in South Korea is increasing four times as rapidly as the population. This probably rivals the rate of increase in the church of the first century. The South Korean church has become God's call to the worldwide body of Christ to make prayer the main business of the church.

Our *Destined for the Throne* Prayer Tower is an effort to reproduce the South Korean prayer burden in this nation. To this end we invite every believer to unite in an exclusive prayer chain of intercessors, agreeing to make *prayer the main business of your lives.* As a token of this dedication you are urged to pledge one hour a day in prayer for worldwide revival. We request that you include the ministry of TBN, since the sole reason for the operation of this growing Network is worldwide revival and soul winning.

As occasion arises and justifies, TBN will endeavor to prepare and mail to each One-hour Intercessor a prayer tape detailing exclusive, confidential information and prayer burdens concerning TBN, its significant new plans, developments, and expansion program. This tape will be mailed only to those who sincerely and conscientiously assume the responsibility of a One-Hour Intercessor. Each such Intercessor will receive an engraved and autographed certificate of membership. All who feel led to assume this solemn responsibility are requested to inform us, giving your name and address. Please write to: TBN—Prayer Tower, P.O. Box A, Santa Ana, CA 92711.

TRINITY BROADCASTING NETWORK

is an all-Christian television network broadcasting the
Gospel 24 hours a day by satellite on:

Channel 40   Southern California
Channel 21   Phoenix, Arizona
Channel 14   Oklahoma City, Okla.
Channel 45   Miami, Florida
Channel 57   Denver, Colorado

Plus nearly 300 Cable Systems